Miniature Schnauzer

A Pet Care Guide for Miniature Schnauzer

General Info, Purchasing, Care, Cost, Keeping, Health, Supplies, Food, Breeding and More Included!

By Lolly Brown

Copyrights and Trademarks

All rights reserved. No part of this book may be reproduced or transformed in any form or by any means, graphic, electronic, or mechanical, including photocopying, recording, taping, or by any information storage retrieval system, without the written permission of the author.

This publipupion is Copyright ©2018 NRB Publishing, an imprint. Nevada. All products, graphics, publipupions, software and services mentioned and recommended in this publipupion are protected by trademarks. In such instance, all trademarks & copyright belong to the respective owners. For information consult www.NRBpublishing.com

Disclaimer and Legal Notice

This product is not legal, medical, or accounting advice and should not be interpreted in that manner. You need to do your own due-diligence to determine if the content of this product is right for you. While every attempt has been made to verify the information shared in this publipupion, neither the author, neither publisher, nor the affiliates assume any responsibility for errors, omissions or contrary interpretation of the subject matter herein. Any perceived slights to any specific person(s) or organization(s) are purely unintentional.

We have no control over the nature, content and availability of the web sites listed in this book. The inclusion of any web site links does not necessarily imply a recommendation or endorse the views expressed within them. We take no responsibility for, and will not be liable for, the websites being temporarily unavailable or being removed from the internet.

The accuracy and completeness of information provided herein and opinions stated herein are not guaranteed or warranted to produce any particular results, and the advice and strategies, contained herein may not be suitable for every individual. Neither the author nor the publisher shall be liable for any loss incurred as a consequence of the use and applipupion, directly or indirectly, of any information presented in this work. This publipupion is designed to provide information in regard to the subject matter covered.

Neither the author nor the publisher assume any responsibility for any errors or omissions, nor do they represent or warrant that the ideas, information, actions, plans, suggestions contained in this book is in all cases accurate. It is the reader's responsibility to find advice before putting anything written in this book into practice. The information in this book is not intended to serve as legal, medical, or accounting advice.

Foreword

The Miniature Schnauzer is known to be the little furry companion that got it all for you. It is intelligent, affectionate, humorous, extrovert, and the personality that is bigger than he is. They have a pleasant, playful, yet alert attitude that could help your build a happy and well-secured home.

Miniature Schnauzers vary greatly in their personality. Some of them are goofballs, some are serious, some are introverted, while some are extroverted, others are sweeter than your typical terrier dog. Their personality varies greatly on how you train it to be. We have yet to explore the mysterious world of the Miniature Schnauzer.

In this book, we will give you everything you need to know about the Miniature Schnauzer. You will learn a lot of things, such as its basic information, feeding, nutrition, health, and breeding concerns.

Let us start our journey and learn about these wonderful furry creatures!

Table of Contents

Introduction 1
Chapter One: Early Beginnings of the Miniature Schnauzer 3
    The Starting Point 4
        Quick Facts 7
Chapter Two: Your Very Own Miniature Schnauzer 11
    Are Miniature Schnauzers Great Pet? 12
    Choosing the Miniature Schnauzer as Your Pet 13
    Male or Female? Which One Should I Choose? 15
    Money Matters 17
    Financial Needs 17
Chapter Three: Picking Your Mini Schnauzer 25
    Puppy or Adult Miniature Schnauzer? 26
Chapter Four: The Miniature Schnauzer's Home 39
Chapter Five: What Does A Miniature Schnauzer Need? 45
    When is the best time to feed my dog? 54
Chapter Six: How to Train My Miniature Schnauzer 57
Chapter Seven: Miniature Schnauzer as Show Dogs 67
Chapter Eight: Grooming My Pet Miniature Schnauzer 75
Chapter Nine: My Miniature Schnauzer's Medical Needs .. 89
Quick Summary and Care Sheet 101
    Basic Information for Miniature Schnauzer 102

Home Requirements	103
Nutritional Needs	104
Glossary of Pup Terms	107
Index	113
Photo Credits	123
References	125

Introduction

The Miniature Schnauzer is a great home companion especially for novice dog owners. They have the attitude that is bigger than their bodies. This dog has a happy outlook that would certainly cheer you up whenever you are sad.

Miniature Schnauzer has a lot of temperament so make sure you can deal with them! They love long walks and enjoyable exercises. However, your pet only wants to be part of the family. Make sure your pet has a companion during the day to play games with.

These little dogs make great watchdog, however, you must train your dog how to act around strangers. Some

Introduction

might be too enthusiastic, while some are a bit of standoffish.

This beloved furry creature plays well with other pets, he might chase the cat, but it is just doing it for fun. However, strange dogs of the same sex are not really great of your Miniature Schnauzer.

This dog loves attention; however, it has a mind on its own and displays resistance when walking on the list. But do not fret; your dog does well on obedience training. Aside from that, this breed is easy to adapt to new environment and could be a great travelling companion. We have lots of information that will help you in taking care of your chosen breed. We start from the basic information up to the health concerns that you need to know.

Have fun in this wild yet interesting journey in the life of the Miniature Schnauzer!

Chapter One: Early Beginnings of the Miniature Schnauzer

The Miniature Schnauzer, also known as Mini Schnauzer, was used to wipe out rats and other pests on German farms for many centuries. However, they made great family dogs from the beginning until now.

Although you might say that they are intelligent and alert dogs, these dogs are a great house companion - they can follow rules and train easily. They have a lot of energy which they use to run around the house as fast as they could. Aside from the given traits, these furry creatures love to play a classic game of tug-of-war. They love to obey and depend on their humans. They can also be kept indoors or outdoors, as they can easily adapt to new environment, you

Chapter One: Early Beginnings of the Miniature Schnauzer

can them as good guard dogs because they will alert you whenever there is an intruder.

Although there are a lot of positive things about this breed, just like other dogs, they have health issues that you need to be concerned. We will tackle the health issues in the later chapter of this book.

In our book, we will be detailing you with a lot of information about the Miniature Schnauzer. We will start with the basic information up to the basic day-to-day needs that will help and guard you in taking care of your chosen dog. This book is essential starting from the purchase until the day it grows up.

The Starting Point

Among all the dogs belonging to the terrier group, the Miniature Schnauzer is the only dog not originating from the Great Britain. This breed originated from Germany, and some existing photos show that this Mini Schnauzer exist as far as the fifteenth century.

'Pinscher' was the name for the standard sized Schnauzer, but was later on changed to 'schnauzer' from the word 'schnauze' or snout. Its name was changed because of the heavy whiskers on the muzzle of the dogs.

Chapter One: Early Beginnings of the Miniature Schnauzer

It is believed that the Miniature Schnauzer is a cross between the Wurttenberg cattle dog and a Standard Poodle or a Spitz. The Miniature Schnauzer's coat characteristics can be lifted between these crosses.

Previously, the standard and miniature schnauzer were born in the same family. The breed was initially used as herding and cattle dogs but was not hunters like the other terriers in England.

In 1897, the first Schnauzers were put into a show, and were named Wirehaired Pinschers, which set the standard size for the breed. Pinscher-Schnauzer Klub was formed in 1895; it listed different kinds of dog such as the Wirehaired Miniature Pinscher that was later on renamed as the Miniature Schnauzer.

In October 1888, the first Miniature Schnauzer was all black, this dog was all black. However, there are also pepper, tan, salt, black, and yellow listed. The different dogs within the Klub were bred together as well as crossing from the different breed to produce new kind of breeds.

In 1920, the first set of dogs was brought to the United States. However, there is no clear difference between the standard and miniature one, and was believed to be the same - so they were shown together. The Wirehaired Pinscher Club of America was formed in 1925 but the two kinds of Schnauzer were not separated until 1926.

Chapter One: Early Beginnings of the Miniature Schnauzer

Recently

After the World War II, the Miniature Schnauzer was popular in United States. This breed, small yet spunky, gets along well with children and adults alike and loves to be with other people.

In 1927, the first Miniature Schnauzer was seen in Canada. It became popular as a companion dog yet still belonging to the terrier type. The first Miniature Schnauzer was registered to the Canadian Kennel Club in 1933, under the breed Schnauzer-Pinscher.

By this time, the breed has become a recognized and well-known breed in the world. There had been a lot of Miniature Schnauzer clubs almost in every country, because this breed works well in the show ring and agility tests.

This breed has the same natural instincts and hunting abilities like their terrier family. These dogs are naturally intelligent and you, as a breeder, should maintain its intelligence as well as its natural curiosity and other notable characteristics.

Recently, breeders began experimenting and forming a new kind of Schnauzer and calling them as "Toy Schnauzer", however, these are not recognized the registry and not sold by any reputable breeder. This small and undersized Miniature Schnauzer has a lot of health

Chapter One: Early Beginnings of the Miniature Schnauzer

condition that affected their growth and will cause more problems and difficulties.

Quick Facts

Origin: Germany

Pedigree:

Breed Size: small size

Body Type and Appearance: The Miniature Schnauzer can be seen as 'square' in proportion. The length of their body is almost equal to the height.

Group: classified as Terrier Group in the American Kennel Club (AKC) as well as the Canadian Kennel Club (CKC); classified as utility group in other kennel club

Height: 30 cm - 36 cm for both male and female.

Weight: 5.4 - 8.2 kg for female, 5.4 - 9.1 kg for male

Coat Length: thick and double

Coat Texture: wiry and fairly coarse

Color: brindle, white, black, fawn, blue, red

Temperament: fearless, spirited, obedient, alert, intelligent, friendly, friendly, smart, active

Strangers: will depend on the training you will give

Chapter One: Early Beginnings of the Miniature Schnauzer

Other Dogs: some might attack, some might be friendly

Other Pets: depends well on the training of the owner

Training: loves to be trained by their humans

Exercise Needs: needs daily exercise

Health Conditions: almost all are healthy but may be affected by the following illnesses: von willebrand's disease, anesthesia sensitivity, deafness, and other eye diseases.

Lifespan: average 12 to 14 years

What's So Special about the Miniature Schnauzer?

- ✓ Loves to play and spend time with people
- ✓ Enjoy the companionship of their humans
- ✓ Needs to be socialized early to have a harmonious relationship with other dogs and animals.
- ✓ Sounds like an old man barking
- ✓ Good with children, but should be monitored during the socialization stage
- ✓ Loves to travel with their family
- ✓ Loves to play fetch and hide-and-seek
- ✓ They can exercise in a small pace, but still require good walk.

Chapter One: Early Beginnings of the Miniature Schnauzer

- ✓ Contains only a minimal amount of grooming
- ✓ Can retain puppy behavior until its adult stage

These are just some of the basic information you need to know about the Miniature Schnauzer. This information is vital if you want to own this breed. However, the journey is just beginning. There is a lot of information you need to know about this breed - especially to keep it happy and very healthy. Let's continue the wonderful journey

Chapter One: Early Beginnings of the Miniature Schnauzer

Chapter Two: Your Very Own Miniature Schnauzer

In the previous chapter, we have discussed the past and recent events about the Miniature Schnauzer. However, that information is not enough for you to take care of your dog. In this case, we will be diving further into the world of the Miniature Schnauzer.

Although Miniature Schnauzer is 'miniature', this breed has all the characteristics that you need to have a happy and healthy household. The breed is great with children, they are naturally intelligent and curious, and only needs minimal grooming. If these are the dog characteristics you are looking for - the Miniature Schnauzer is great for you!

Chapter Two: Your Very Own Miniature Schnauzer

In the succeeding pages, we will be dealing in why the Miniature Schnauzer is the best pet for you. We will be giving you information on its temperament, behaviour towards other pets, and other relevant information.

Are Miniature Schnauzers Great Pet?

There are a lot of considerations before you decide on what breed is right for you. There are a lot of characteristics and factors you need to look out for before you buy your first pet, you should know all the things about your pet before you buy it.

Miniature Schnauzers are little dogs with big personalities. In this case, if you are up for hours of fun and training - this dog is great for you! You can have great company that deals well with children and other guests. Let us continue knowing our favourite fury creature.

Temperament

The Miniature Schnauzer is classified as a terrier in the United States and Canada; they do not have the necessary terrier temperament.

A Miniature Schnauzer is friendly and obedient; it should not be overly aggressive and timid. If you do not

Chapter Two: Your Very Own Miniature Schnauzer

train your dog at an early age, your dog could be very aggressive towards other people or animals.

Just like any other small dogs, Miniature Schnauzers do not know that they are miniature. They will tend to growl and fight off larger dogs, which could somehow lead to fights. You can avoid these instances through obedience training and proper socialization.

Choosing the Miniature Schnauzer as Your Pet

In this part, we will be giving you the positive and negative traits of the Miniature Schnauzer. You need to go through these one by one, and think if you can handle the traits. If not, go find another breed. If yes, continue your journey for this breed.

Here are the characteristics of the Miniature Schnauzer:

Chapter Two: Your Very Own Miniature Schnauzer

Positive Traits

- Small sized
- Sturdy yet still athletic
- Its coat does not shed too much
- Has a wise expression through its whiskery face
- Makes a great watchdog
- Polite with guests
- Generally good with other pets

Negative Traits

- Needs enough exercise throughout the day
- Needs to have interesting activities to fight off boredom
- Needs a companion throughout the day.
- Needs enough socialization or else it will get suspicious or distrusting to people around it.
- Can chase other animals
- Stubborn
- Can bark too much
- You need to have it groom every now and then
- Can have a wide variety of temperament, since the Miniature Schnauzer has a lot of history

Chapter Two: Your Very Own Miniature Schnauzer

Male or Female? Which One Should I Choose?

Another decision you need to do is to choose whether you want a male or female dog. Each gender has its own characteristics; you need to know these things because you need to find the ones that will match you the most.

You should not just choose the 'cutest' or the most 'behave' puppy or dog in the bunch. Determine the gender and characteristics that will best match you and your family's personality.

MALES

- ✓ Generally larger and heavier
- ✓ Eats more food than the non-pregnant counterpart
- ✓ More aggressive and independent
- ✓ Some male dogs are more difficult to manage in small, confined areas
- ✓ Some of them do not go well with other male dogs, especially if there are other female that is in heat.
- ✓ Forms a closer bond with only one person
- ✓ Quicker to develop sexually than its counterpart
- ✓ Males will roam and find female in heat

- ✓ Will become possessive of the female, even their owners.
- ✓ Some might even be aggressive towards the female especially if it is not receptive to its advances
- ✓ Some might be even difficult to train and more independent.
- ✓ Requires more exercise and friskier
- ✓ May be difficult to socialize with other dogs and animals, you need to begin socialization early.

FEMALES

- ✓ Smaller than male dogs
- ✓ Less aggressive
- ✓ Mothers are as protective as the males
- ✓ Less excitable
- ✓ Easier to train
- ✓ Can be shy or cowed if treated badly or scolded in an angry tone
- ✓ Less protective than the males
- ✓ Some might fight with female counterpart
- ✓ Females will establish a hierarchy and develop a pecking order.

Chapter Two: Your Very Own Miniature Schnauzer

How Are They The Same?

- ✓ Needs the same amount of time and attention
- ✓ Needs the same amount of exercise, general care, and love.
- ✓ Needs veterinary check-ups and yearly vaccination.

Money Matters

Purchasing your first pet is a big responsibility. There are a lot of things you need to take care for. It does not only end in buying your pet, it also includes a lot of expenses for its growth and happiness.

In this portion, we will give you an insight on the money matters about your pet. These are only rough estimates and some prices might be higher or lower than its original price. Make sure you are financially prepared in every endeavour.

Financial Needs

There are a lot of things you need to prepare before you bring home your first pet. Bringing in your first pet will surely change your household budget.

Chapter Two: Your Very Own Miniature Schnauzer

You need to allot money for food, grooming, toys, and treats. This will ensure that your dog will be happy. You can even provide a budget plan so you can track and know all the expenses that you will have in the future. Remember, your expenses will start in purchasing your dog but will not stop there. You might be overwhelmed at first, but you can adjust to it quickly.

You can control your expenses through choosing the cheapest price possible. However, you need to make sure that the things you buy is strong enough to last long for your dog, you should not buy accessories made of cheap material.

We will help you create a budget plan for your Miniature Schnauzer.

Things I Need to Purchase:

✓ Miniature Schnauzer

Miniature Schnauzer is a great breed because they are the best extrovert breed in the canine group. Many people like to have them as pets, sometimes; this is the cause of the price inflation.

Typically, you need to spend around $500 to $2700 if you want your own Miniature Schnauzer. However, if you want to have a show dog, the price will be higher. You do

Chapter Two: Your Very Own Miniature Schnauzer

not need to worry about finding the breed because it is easily available in many pet shops or breeders.

✓ Dog Bed/ Dog Crate

Buying a dog bed or dog crate may be called a luxury, however, you would want your dog to have its own space and be at peace especially at night.

You can buy him a dog bed for comfort. Since your dog is only a small sized dog, you can buy a medium sized bed for him. This medium sized bed will be used by your pet from its puppy stage until its adult stage.

You may need to spend around $20 to $50 for the bed. Remember, the price depends on the quality and brand of the bed.

✓ Toys

Miniature Schnauzers are active little puppers. They love to play around the house during dull moments. It is best that you keep them occupied through various toys.

However, you should not buy a lot of toys for your dog, as your dog could not enjoy them all at once.

Chapter Two: Your Very Own Miniature Schnauzer

- ✓ Grooming Tools

Miniature Schnauzer is a good looking dog breed that has a long beard, moustache, and bushy eyebrows which make them outstanding among all other breeds.

All of this fur makes them a little difficult to groom, you need to properly clean and groom them to keep its fur from tangling.

Here are the essential things you need to buy for your Miniature Schnauzer:

- ✓ Electric Clipper for dog paws
- ✓ Slicker Brush
- ✓ Detangle Solutions
- ✓ Flea Comb
- ✓ Dog Bath
- ✓ Medium or Wide-Tooth Comb

We will go into detail on how much you need to spend on these brushes on the succeeding chapters in this book. Read on to know more!

Chapter Two: Your Very Own Miniature Schnauzer

- ✓ Dog Food and Treats

Dog Food and Treats are essential for your dog's growth and health. You need to buy the best possible brand of dog food that will ensure your dog's health and nutrition. In the succeeding chapters, we will help you find the best brand of dog food and how to find the nutritional facts in the brand.

Other than that, dog treats are important for training your dog. You can use these as rewards for your dog during obedience training. Dog treats have also other health benefits such as cleaning your dog's teeth and giving your dog's nutritional needs.

Other Essentials:

- ✓ Medical Expenses

Medical expenses are inevitable to anyone. Just like humans, dog get sick due to unfortunate incidents. You might think it is not a great idea to save for your dog's medical needs. However, you do not know when you need to rush your dog to the ER.

Chapter Two: Your Very Own Miniature Schnauzer

- ✓ Micro-Chipping

Micro-chipping is an option that will help you save your pet every time it gets lost. As the name implies, a micro-chip is inserted under the dog's skin. This micro-chip contains the owner's information and contact number.

You might think that a micro-chip is not that necessary, however, if your dog ever gets lost, the micro-chip could help your dog return to you safely and easily.

- ✓ Vaccinations

Vaccines are important especially for puppies. There are a lot of mandated vaccines and boosters that you need to get for you puppy.

These vaccines are important to protect your puppy from various diseases and illnesses, and although the mother could give the necessary anti-bodies for the puppy to grow happy and healthy, but this is not enough to protect the puppy in the distant future.

- ✓ Spay/Neuter Surgery

Spay and Neuter Surgery is an option that you can choose for your pet. Spay/Neuter Surgery can prevent unwanted pregnancy and production of many litters.

Chapter Two: Your Very Own Miniature Schnauzer

The Spay and Neuter Surgery would stop the female to be in heat and the male to find women that is in heat.

✓ Vet Consultation

Vet consultations are very important in the life of a pet. You need to have initial vet consultation to know if your pet is great condition. These vet consultations would entail getting the shots and boosters as well as clipping the nails of your dog. You should visit your vet at least two times a year or more if you have purchased your dog at an early age.

These are some of the things you need to look out for if you want to take care of a Miniature Schnauzer and for it to have a happy and healthy life.

There are other things you need to know about your pet, let's continue our journey to have a happy and healthy pet

Chapter Two: Your Very Own Miniature Schnauzer

Chapter Three: Picking Your Mini Schnauzer

In this chapter, we will be telling you the difference among the different kinds of Miniature Schnauzer you can purchase. You can buy this breed as a puppy or adult, male or female, each category has its own advantages and disadvantages. We will help you decide what kind you want to purchase.

Aside from this, we will be listing down the characteristics of a reputable breeder as well as some sites that will help you in your Miniature Schnauzer concerns.

Chapter Three: Picking Your Mini Schnauzer

Puppy or Adult Miniature Schnauzer?

There are a lot of things you need to consider before you want to buy an adult or puppy Miniature Schnauzer. Make sure you are really committed in this relationship before you purchase your first dog. Here are some questions you need to answer:

- ✓ Am I capable of training a puppy?
- ✓ How much time could I give to my puppy for training?
- ✓ Can I be with my puppy in most parts of the day and night?
- ✓ Am I patient with puppies?

In the upcoming section, we will be giving you the advantages and disadvantages of purchasing your puppy or adult Miniature Schnauzer. Make sure you think these things through especially consider your environment and situation.

Chapter Three: Picking Your Mini Schnauzer

ADVANTAGES OF A PUPPY MINIATURE SCHNAUZER

- ✓ A puppy will be a cute and lovable additional member of your family.

- ✓ Puppies are a great addition for individuals and families that want to have a younger animal inside their house.

- ✓ You can provide your own training and socialization for the puppy. This will ensure that you will have a healthy, happy, and well-behaved dog.

- ✓ If you have bought the Miniature Schnauzer from a reputable breeder, you can be sure that the dog will stay with you for the longest time possible. You should also give the best care, nutrition, and vet treatment.

DISADVANTAGES OF A MINIATURE SCHNAUZER PUPPY

- ✓ You need to provide a lot of time and effort to successfully train your puppy. This can be very difficult to manage especially those who have a job and a family to raise every day.

- ✓ A Miniature Schnauzer puppy is like a newborn, especially for the first few months. You need to be there twenty four hours a day, seven days a week.

Chapter Three: Picking Your Mini Schnauzer

- ✓ You need to socialize your puppy to new environment and animals.

- ✓ Puppies go through difficult stages; you may need to protect your household items unless you want to to be destroyed or broken.

- ✓ You need to spend time housebreaking your pet. There are a lot of techniques to housebreak your pet, but it depends on how you raise it.

- ✓ You may not know the whole history of the family and the puppy if you had gotten it from the shelter.

You can also purchase an adult Miniature Schnauzer. Here, we will give you the advantages and disadvantages of this category.

ADVANTAGES OF AN ADULT MINIATURE SCHNAUZER

- ✓ You can choose the size, temperament, behavior, and appearance of the dog.

- ✓ Adult dogs are already housebroken and trained, which can save time, patience, and household items.

- ✓ Adult dogs know how to behave well inside a house, this will lessen training time.

Chapter Three: Picking Your Mini Schnauzer

- ✓ They are less stressed and calmer when in a new environment.

- ✓ Responses well to commands.

DISADVANTAGES OF AN ADULT MINIATURE SCHNAUZER

✓ Some adult Miniature Schnauzers carry the bad habits they have learned from their previous owners. You may re-train the dog for it to behave in an acceptable way.

✓ Adult Miniature Schnauzer may require a period of adjustment in their new environment, so they might not listen to you at first. You need to give attention and time to fully bond with your dog and your family.

✓ Adult dogs may have a difficulty in socializing with other animals; you need to give attention in introducing your dog with other pets.

These are just some of the points that you need to consider if you want to purchase an adult or puppy. Either if you want to purchase an adult or puppy dog, you need to give it attention and love, if you have given these two requirements - your dog will immediately feel at home and be a part of the family.

Chapter Three: Picking Your Mini Schnauzer

Buying My Own Miniature Schnauzer

If you have already decided that you want a puppy or adult dog, you need now to decide where to buy the pet. There are a lot of considerations on where you get your pet. Here are some options that you can choose from:

RESCUE SHELTER

This is a good option if you want to have an adult Miniature Schnauzer. The shelter could give you time to bond with the dog before purchasing it, in this time; you can check its behaviour and temperament.

Some shelters may even agree that you can return the dog if it has not adjusted well at your home. If you plan to get your pet from the shelter, be sure to:

- ✓ Have all the information about the pet.
- ✓ Make sure that the dog is completely vaccinated and has an updated check-up
- ✓ Know if the dog has behavioural issues such as overeating or barking.
- ✓ Look for the signs of lethargic.
- ✓ Spend time with the dog before the purchase

Chapter Three: Picking Your Mini Schnauzer

- ✓ Check the policy on neutering or spaying.
- ✓ Returning the dog if it has not adjusted well.

However, there are still disadvantages if you will get your Miniature Schnauzer from a shelter. These are:

- ✓ The dog might have bad behaviors and you might need to re-train them.
- ✓ Shelters, often, have limited breeding, gender, and size.
- ✓ You will not truly know the lineage or history of the breed.
- ✓ You will settle for an adult Miniature Schnauzer.
- ✓ You might have to agree to have your dog neutered or spayed before leaving the shelter.

PET STORES

Pet stores are one of the first choices when buying a dog. Some stores offer both pure-bred and cross-bred puppies and even adults. You can choose the color, breed, and sex that you want to acquire in a pet store. However, you can't be really sure if the dog is a pure breed and is taken care properly. Many dogs from the pet store are from the 'puppy mills' which produces many dogs at once. Other than that, employees do not know the entire history of the dog that you want to buy.

Chapter Three: Picking Your Mini Schnauzer

You can't really know, too, the true behaviour of the dog, as it does not have enough littermates. Finally, some might even contract diseases due to the environment that they are in.

BREEDER

This might be the most expensive choice, but this could yield you the best option possible. Most breeders will give you a purebred puppy, especially if it came from a reputable breeder.

Most breeders would assure you great health as well as the history of the breed. In turn to this, the breeder would want to interview and get to know you as the potential owner of his puppies. Reputable breeders would want you to personally inspect the litter before choosing the best pup for you.

Other than that, reputable breeders will recommend you food, vets, training equipment, and problems. Other than that, you will learn a lot from the breeder.

Before you visit the breeder, make sure you have enough information about the breed as well as possible health information about the breed that you want to buy. You can counter check the breeder if s/he has enough information about the dog.

Chapter Three: Picking Your Mini Schnauzer

You should remember that finding show or champion dogs are more difficult than purebred dogs and somehow pricier. Buying your Miniature Schnauzer from a breeder will help you understand its temperament and lineage, as well as its medical background.

Finding the Reputable Miniature Schnauzer Breeder

First thing that you need to consider for the breeder is the love and affection it give to the dog. The breeder focuses on the dog's interests rather than his own. However, some breeder has only money in mind in selling their Miniature Schnauzer.

Here are some guidelines on why you should get a puppy from a Miniature Schnauzer Breeder:

- ✓ You get peace of mind as you will know the medical history of the puppy's health and its parents.
- ✓ You can be sure that the puppy will meet the specification and breed standards.
- ✓ The breeder can understand your needs.
- ✓ You can ask the breeder for vaccine, medical concerns, as well as other questions for raising the puppy.

Chapter Three: Picking Your Mini Schnauzer

What Should I Ask the Miniature Schnauzer Breeder?

Breeders want their dog's lineage to continue, they want to know that their dogs are being cared of, probably they will help you in every query that you have.

You should ask these questions to your Miniature Schnauzer breeder:

✓ Do you have a contract to purchase that guarantees that this breed is of great health and a refund or return policy?

✓ Have you worked with both of the dog's parents?

✓ Can you give me a lineage of the dog going back to generations?

✓ Can I see other animals in the kennel?

✓ Can I see if the puppies and adults are socialized together?

✓ Do you have a limit on the puppy production?

✓ Do any clubs or organizations recognize you as a breeder?

✓ How often you breed the male and female Miniature Schnauzer?

A reputable Miniature Schnauzer breeder will be concerned to the new owner of his or her Miniature Schnauzer puppy. S/he will only talk to serious buyers and

Chapter Three: Picking Your Mini Schnauzer

refuse connection if you are not that responsible. You might not even interact with the breed if you are just inquiring about the breed.

WHAT WILL THE MINIATURE SCHNAUZER BREEDER ASK ME?

First time buyers would often be overwhelmed with all of things they need to know before even buying the pet. However, these steps are necessary to ensure that you will get the best puppy and you can give great care and treatment for it.

Here are some things that the Miniature Schnauzer breeder may ask you:

- ✓ How does your home look like? Some breeder may even want to visit your home just as you will visit their home for inspection.
- ✓ What do you want to plan to do with the dog? The breeder might even suggest spaying or neutering the dog or advise you to breed the animal if only they approve.
- ✓ The breeder might even ask for your pet's history, how many pets you have had and how you took care of them.
- ✓ Some breeder might want their litter to be trained at a certain trainer or only using a specific method.

Chapter Three: Picking Your Mini Schnauzer

- ✓ Some breeder might want you to return to them the dog if you plan to sell it in the future, in case you changed your mind in taking care of the dog.

This information is important in acquiring your dog. Make sure you have enough info before you go off and buy your first pet.

The Healthy Miniature Schnauzer

Choosing a healthy breed is important. You might be attached to this dog so you might want it to be in its best form and healthiest state as possible.

Some dogs might even cost you a lot of money for vet consultations, and you might not even afford some of it. Aside from the financial struggle, you might even have to deal with the emotional struggle of a sick pet that could possibly lead to death.

Before you choose that specific dog from the litter, here are the signs of a healthy puppy of dog:

- ✓ Clear bright eyes, which will follow you whenever yo move.
- ✓ Quick responses to new sounds or weird noises.
- ✓ No discharge from mouth, ears, eyes.

Chapter Three: Picking Your Mini Schnauzer

- ✓ Squeaky clean smell of puppy breath.

- ✓ Healthy looking teeth and gums that is pink and firm.

- ✓ Your chosen dog should not be over timid or aggressive, distant to the litter and people around it.

- ✓ The dog should be able to walk and move without lameness or stiffness.

- ✓ The stomach should not be swollen or distended. There should not be a discomfort when pressed.

- ✓ Your dog should have good appetite and wants food.

- ✓ The dog should not be too heavy or too thin.

- ✓ The coat should be in great condition and free from any rashes.

- ✓ The Miniature Schnauzer can be petted once you have established the relationship.

Chapter Three: Picking Your Mini Schnauzer

Chapter Four: The Miniature Schnauzer's Home

Miniature Schnauzers are wonderful little creatures. They are small dogs with very big attitudes. They can be a bit overwhelming at first, but you will get a hang of it soon enough. There are a lot of things you need to learn for your dog. You need to give time and effort to knowing these things before you dive into the world of Miniature Schnauzer.

Your first day with your pet will be very exciting yet scary process. You might be scared into taking care from day one, but we will help you every step of the way to the right path into taking care of the dog.

Chapter Four: The Miniature Schnauzer's Home

Bringing Home a Miniature Schnauzer Puppy

One of the best feelings in the world is bringing a Miniature Schnauzer puppy at home; however, people do not really know how challenging bringing a puppy is. You need to carefully set up your home before your bring your Miniature Schnauzer home, this is to prevent frustration, damaging of several items, and creating a safe environment for the puppy and your family.

You need to puppy proof your home to avoid any incidents and ensure that you can give proper introduction of the puppy to the litter and the family.

You need to ready all the supplies. Other than this, you need to be eager to work and care for your puppy, also, you give your dog a space to stay, and keep a strict schedule for exercise and feeding. Further, you need to research on training methods for your puppy.

The Needed Supplies

There are a lot of supplies you need to buy to ensure that your dog will feel at home. You may need to talk to your breeder and ask him or her things does he or she recommend. Here are some basic supplies you need to buy:

- ✓ This book. You need to use this book religiously because we will be giving you a lot of information for health,

Chapter Four: The Miniature Schnauzer's Home

training methods, and care. But, you can also ask your breeder what book s/he uses.

- ✓ Dog crate. You might want to purchase a dog crate for easy transport. Make sure you buy the crate one size larger for your dog.

- ✓ Dog bed. Make sure you buy a dog bed with comfortable bedding that could not be easily destroyed or chewed. Also, make sure that the bedding is washable, as you may need to clean it more than once.

- ✓ Puppy collar. A collar is a special tool for your puppy. This collar could help you especially if your puppy likes to run around especially outside. Make sure than this collar is woven or made of soft fabric. You should not buckle the collar too tight.

- ✓ Identification Tag. An identification tag can be micro-chipped into your dog's skin. This tag contains information about the owner.

- ✓ Grooming supplies. There are several grooming supplies needed by the Miniature Schnauzer.

- ✓ Toys. Toys are important for recreation and training. You can keep your Miniature Schnauzer occupied through toys. However, the plastic parts should not be swallowed by the dog. Remember, if your dog is occupied, s/he will not have time to chew and destroy your household items.

Chapter Four: The Miniature Schnauzer's Home

- ✓ Food. You need to supply your dog with adequate quality dog food. Ask the breeder his/her recommendation or even ask the seller the kind of food a puppy needs for growth. Also, you need to change the food often as your dog's needs differ throughout its life. However, you should only change the food at small amount to prevent sudden shocks for the dog and its digestive system.

- ✓ Food and Water Bowl. Food and water bowls are important for your dog. Make sure you have a stainless steel or a hard plastic. Your puppy needs clean water almost every day.

Puppy Proofing Your Home

A puppy is just like a new baby, it is important to have a safe home environment. Puppies love to run around and get nosey about everything, especially in a new environment. Here are some puppy proofing checks you need to do:

- ✓ Keep all the cords and strings. Even a small string can be dangerous to your puppy and may cause problems for your dog.

- ✓ Keep away all the small objects.

Chapter Four: The Miniature Schnauzer's Home

- ✓ Make sure that your houseplants are not poisonous. Remove them from your room and make sure your dog has no access for it.

- ✓ Keep electrical cords away from the dog. If you can't keep the cord away from the dog, make sure you treat it with a no-chew spray to make it unpleasant for them.

Welcoming Your Adult Miniature Schnauzer at Home

Bringing an adult Miniature Schnauzer is different from having a puppy at your house. An adult Miniature Schnauzer is already housebroken but should be trained inside the house and behaving appropriately. However, you might still need some things you need to prepare for your dog.

Basic Supplies

These basic supplies are needed before your dog even comes home. Make sure you have this in stock whenever your dog needs it:

- ✓ Food and Water Bowl. Make sure it will not tip easily and sturdy.

- ✓ Kennel or Dog Crate. This is only an option but needed if you want to transport your dog easily.

Chapter Four: The Miniature Schnauzer's Home

- ✓ Dog Bed. A safe space is needed by your dog, to call its own.

- ✓ Food. Make sure your dog has good quality dry dog food for your dog. This will ensure that your dog will have the best nutrients at the cheapest price..

These are just some of the basic need you need to prepare for your dog's first day. There are a lot of things you need to prepare throughout the lifespan of the dog. Let's continue our journey and learn more!

Chapter Five: What Does A Miniature Schnauzer Need?

Miniature Schnauzers are great home companion. These terrific small dogs love companion but somehow resistant to training, you need to show authority at an early age to teach your dog how to behave.

Just like any living being, your Miniature Schnauzer has a lot of needs you need to take care of. You need to provide these things because your dog can't provide these things on its own. Make sure you give enough of these things to your pet Miniature Schnauzer to ensure that your dog will have a happy and healthy life during its stay in your home.

Chapter Five: What Does A Miniature Schnauzer Need?

Exercise Needs

Exercise is important to human health and overall well-being for both human and dogs. Dogs need exercise while some breeds may require more exercise than others.

Here are the reasons why your Miniature Schnauzer needs exercise:

- ✓ It helps them to be more content and stay more alert. Exercise makes their brain work.

- ✓ It makes them sleep better. Dogs with high energy can't sleep early and get enough hours because their brains are still working at night.

- ✓ Exercise makes socialization better. It can help them relate to other dog's needs as well as their human's needs.

- ✓ Exercises can eliminate early signs of diseases which can help your dog live longer and be healthier.

- ✓ It helps to build strong bones and muscles because it sheds off excess fats in their bodies.

- ✓ It improves their cardiovascular system as it strengthens their heart.

Chapter Five: What Does A Miniature Schnauzer Need?

You can start with walks and play activities which can allow them to run and walk around your yard or any enclosed area if you have gotten your Miniature Schnauzer as a puppy. However, you might need to encourage your older Miniature Schnauzer for walks and create exercise programs.

You also need to consider the weight and energy level for the dog and their exercise. Some dogs might only want limited or moderate amount of exercise.

There are several factors that will influence the exercise level needed by your dog:

- ✓ Age. Dogs of different ages require different level of energy. Try having small walks first and have the dog inspect or explore the area. Do not let them run too much or rough play, at any age. If you have more than one Miniature Schnauzer, make sure you walk them separately to ensure that both of them will get the suitable walk for them.

- ✓ Physical Condition. Miniature Schnauzers can be "couch potatoes," make sure you start with a short 15 minute walk twice a day to get started. You can increase the length of the walk and the pace that you are walking. Be on the lookout for any distress in dogs such as wheezing, panting or any respiratory problems. Dogs

Chapter Five: What Does A Miniature Schnauzer Need?

with short noses, such as the Miniature Schnauzer, will have trouble breathing especially when they are running too fast. Make the walks shorter but more frequent. Aside from this, Miniature Schnauzer has short legs, so they only need a shorter walk than longer legged dog. You can have a half hour twice a day walk for your Miniature Schnauzer. However, if your dog is still having difficulty, consult your veterinarian immediately.

- ✓ Variety. Add a little variety for your dog's exercise:
  - Training or obedience class
  - Frisbee chasing
  - Play fetch with a ball
  - Retractable leash
  - Walk in a new park or neighborhood
  - Invite a friend with a dog to walk with
  - Jogging for a few minutes then walking for a few minutes.

Chapter Five: What Does A Miniature Schnauzer Need?

Nutrition Basics

Not all dogs need the same thing, especially when it comes to nutrition. You need to understand the type of diet and nutrition best suited for your dog. Here are some things you need to remember for your Miniature Schnauzer:

OMNIVORES

People think that if animals only eat meat, they are carnivores. However, dogs are omnivores, which mean they love to eat fruits and vegetables. These foods are rich in other nutrients and minerals which the dog needs to grow healthy, have shiny coats, good bones, teeth, and well-developed muscles.

THE DIETARY NEED

Your dog needs the following building blocks, including:

- ✓ Amino acids
- ✓ Vitamins
- ✓ Minerals
- ✓ Fats
- ✓ Carbohydrates

Chapter Five: What Does A Miniature Schnauzer Need?

- ✓ Proteins

If you see negative changes in your dog's skin and body, you may need to examine the food label of the feed that you are currently giving your dog. A vet visit may be necessary so you can know the needed amount of dietary elements for your Miniature Schnauzer.

Avoid food that contains wheat or corn, or anything that has excessive amounts of chemical preservative. To check if the dog food has corn, soak the feed in water for 20 minutes, if it mushes, it contains wheat or corn.

Other than that, check how much protein there is in your food. A slightly inactive dog will need a lower amount of protein. Pregnant females and puppies need special diets to suit their needs.

What Not To Give To My Miniature Schnauzer?

If there are foods you can give your Miniature Schnauzer, there are also foods that you should not give your dog. First, you need to avoid feeding your dog too much human food/ table scraps.

You should only give around 10% of table scraps or human food, or better, you should not really give table scraps to them. Other than that, you should never give supplements and human vitamins to your dog because it might cause some issues.

Chapter Five: What Does A Miniature Schnauzer Need?

Aside from these things, you should never give cheese or yogurt as it may cause diarrhea to some dogs. Cooked bones can easily splinter in the dog's mouth and even cause damage to the throat, gums, and stomach's lining.

In addition to these, the bones may lodge in the throat and may cause severe damage. Raw eggs will cause salmonella, just like in humans. It will also decrease the rate and amount of absorption of biotin, which will diminish the coat quality and hair problems.

Salty or even salty food will cause electrolyte imbalances and dehydration in dogs. This should be eliminated from the diet. Aside from salt, you should also eliminate garlic and onion because they contain sulfoxides and disulfides that will cause anemia to dogs.

Do not feed your dog cat food or any other feeds. Cat food are only made for cats and tend to be high in proteins and sugars, this can cause complication for your dog. In addition, cats and dogs have different dietary needs.

Any raw meat should be avoided by the dog. These meats contain various diseases that will be fatal to your dog if you will not treat it properly. Internal meats, kidney and liver, can be given to your dogs if it is organic because there are many toxins present in these organs.

Chapter Five: What Does A Miniature Schnauzer Need?

Candies and chocolates should also be avoided by the dog. Chocolate can be toxic to your dog, which can be lethal even if taken in small doses. Candies have high amount of sugar that area not healthy for your dog.

Feeding My Miniature Schnauzer

Buying food for your dog is not an easy task, you will be overwhelmed with the big number of dog food available in the shelves, and there are a lot of varieties that you will see there.

You need to take time to read and understand the label together with the needs of your dogs; you will then find the one fitted for your dog's needs.

During its lifetime, you would change the feeding requirement more often than not. Your puppy must be fed at least three times a day until it is four months old, your puppy has a smaller stomach but still needs to eat plenty because it is growing at a very fast pace.

When it reaches the four months of age, you need to decrease its feeding schedule to twice a day. When it reaches adulthood, you only need to feed it once a day or you can free-feed it if they are not over-eaters or likes to stay outside. If you plan to change its feeding schedule, you need to closely monitor the dog and see the effects such as the

Chapter Five: What Does A Miniature Schnauzer Need?

overall health of your dog. Aside from this, you need to provide fresh water.

WET FOOD VS. DRY FOOD

You have a choice to give your dog wet food or dry food, or a combination of both.

Wet Food

- ✓ More palatable for dogs of any ages
- ✓ Better to be fed to too young or too old dog.
- ✓ Dogs with certain diseases or dental problems need to be fed wet food.
- ✓ Does not have the same consistency and fiber as dry food.
- ✓ Dogs that only eat this will produce excessive amounts of gas and may need to poop a lot.

Dry Food

- ✓ Unpalatable for dogs
- ✓ If your dog is on this diet, the food will clean the teeth and promote healthy digestion.

Chapter Five: What Does A Miniature Schnauzer Need?

- ✓ Make sure the dog has access to clean water

- ✓ Read the label and make sure that the ingredient is not corn, corn meal, or wheat as these are fillers that could swell up in your dog's stomach when consumed,

- ✓ Talk to your veterinarian and see if the food is highly recommended.

When is the best time to feed my dog?

There are certain ways to feed your dog. You need to figure out what is the best procedure for your dog to receive its food. Many dogs would require a required schedule.

SCHEDULED FEEDING

Scheduled feeding, as the name implies, is placing the food for the dog for twenty minutes and removed after the time. In this procedure, when the twenty minutes is up, you need to remove the food whether the dog has eaten or not.

This is a great plan especially with indoor dogs as it can help with exercises and trips.

Chapter Five: What Does A Miniature Schnauzer Need?

FREE FEEDING

When you use this technique, you place an automatic feeder or bowl of food for the dog; they may be the ones to access how much they will eat. This is a good technique if your dog is not a glutton and can resist eating much food.

You can try both methods and see what technique is best suited for your dog.

Home Cooking for My Miniature Schnauzer

Cooking is a great way to express your love for your Miniature Schnauzer; this will also ensure that your dog will get fresh, high quality food prepared in a clean and safe environment.

There are many recipes you can follow. Most of these include:

- ✓ Turkey
- ✓ Lean beef
- ✓ Cauliflower
- ✓ Celery
- ✓ Parsley
- ✓ Chicken
- ✓ Beans

Chapter Five: What Does A Miniature Schnauzer Need?

- ✓ Broccoli
- ✓ Zucchini
- ✓ Carrots

Any combination of this food can be fed to your dog. This can last for up to five days. Remember; do not use garlic, onions, or mushrooms in your food as this can cause several reactions to your dog.

These are just some things you need to remember for your dog's need. We need to continue more and explore the world of the Miniature Schnauzer.

Chapter Six: How to Train My Miniature Schnauzer

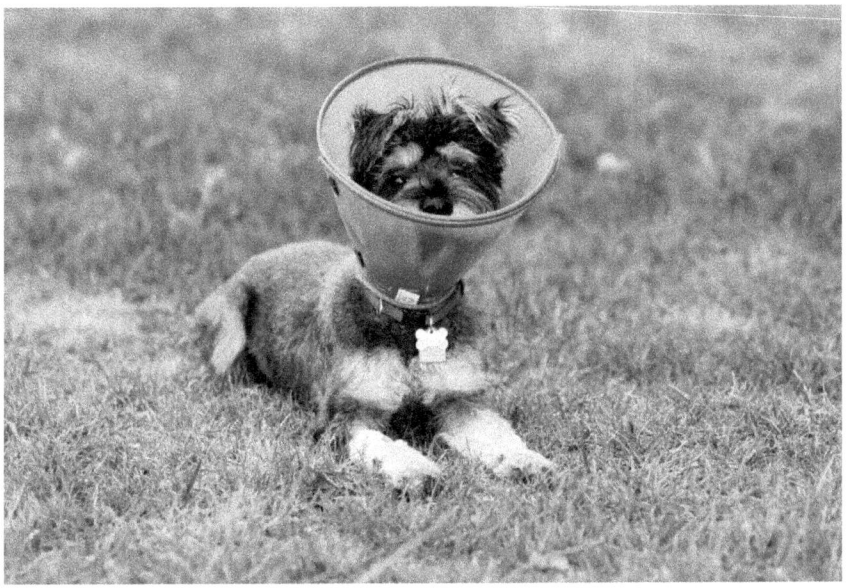

Training your dog is a must, especially during its early days in your home. It must learn how to obey and somehow do some tricks for it to be well-socialized and be obedient to you and your family.

In this chapter, we will give you with a lot of tips and tricks into training your Miniature Schnauzer. Remember, Miniature Schnauzer are fun little individual but it still has a mind on its own, it will run around and play whenever it can! Let's learn how to train our dog.

Chapter Six: Miniature Schnauzer as Show Dogs

Training Your Dog

Training your dog should not be difficult for both you and your dog. You just need to follow these rules and regulations so it will make you and your dog's life easier.

You just need to know in what stage your dog is in so you can give the proper training attitude and scheme for your dog. For this book, we will be dealing with puppies and retraining adult dogs.

However, you should still research the breed and ask other trainers for their input.

Miniature Schnauzers are high-strung and likes to bark. Aside from that, they can be very stubborn but they can still respond to the owner if you are consistent in the training.

Have a Fun Training

- ✓ To have a fun training, make sure you are in an enthusiastic and positive mood.
- ✓ Do not train your dog if you are stressed, tired, or unhappy, this will only stress your dog and make the training more difficult.
- ✓ Give small healthy treats aside from the verbal praises.

Chapter Six: Miniature Schnauzer as Show Dogs

- ✓ Make sure you pet and hug them when you begin the training session.
- ✓ Have a play session after the training session so your dog can feel it can have a reward after a stressful journey.
- ✓ Exercise your pet before training, to burn the excess energy and it helps your dog to focus.
- ✓ Learn how to praise, spend time with your pets, and learn together with your pet.
- ✓ Create a positive environment so you can have a successful training session.

A NATURAL TRAINING

- ✓ Reward your puppy when it urinates or poops in a proper location.
- ✓ Make sure you always praise them whenever they do a good job.

A CONSISTENT TRAINING

- ✓ You need to consistently train your puppy to know its expectations and see if it really likes the training every day.

Chapter Six: Miniature Schnauzer as Show Dogs

- ✓ Teach your housemates the same commands so your dog will not be confused.

- ✓ Tell your housemates of your expectations when you are training your dog; do not strain your strong too much for it not to enjoy the training session.

PATIENCE

- ✓ Miniature Schnauzers are just like babies, they can learn a lot if you will teach them the right commands.

- ✓ You, first, need to housebreak your dog; this is the first thing you need to do, however, this is the hardest.

- ✓ Have exercise breaks in between your training sessions as they need to urinate or poop frequently.

- ✓ Plan activities or training whenever there is the least noise, or the minimum amount of distraction. Make sure you do not have any TV on or any noise that would distract them.

- ✓ Puppies have short attention span; take frequent breaks when you see that your puppy is not focused on the task at hand.

- ✓ Short training is more effective than longer ones.

Chapter Six: Miniature Schnauzer as Show Dogs

DO NOT HIT THE PUPPY

- ✓ Your puppy trusts you when it has human contact with you.

- ✓ If you create a negative human contact with it, its trust and bond with you will weaken.

- ✓ If your dog is afraid of you, it will be very difficult to train; your dog may become too shy or very aggressive.

- ✓ Make use of positive commands or stating a sharp 'NO' rather than a physical punishment.

DO IT HABITUALLY

- ✓ Schedule a routine for your training so your dog can differentiate training and play time.

- ✓ Praise your dog when it responds correctly.

- ✓ Have a positive attitude when training your dog.

- ✓ Be consistent in the command and training style.

- ✓ Understand your dog's characteristics. You can ask a fellow breeder, vet, or trainer.

Chapter Six: Miniature Schnauzer as Show Dogs

Dog Training 101

Your dog should be able to learn these basic commands, sit, stay, down, and come. If your dog has mastered these, you can try to do much more difficult commands.

You can start the training as early as possible, this will allow the Miniature Schnauzer what are the negative behaviour and get rid of them.

When the puppy comes to you when you say 'come' praise and reward the puppy immediately. However, only do this if the dog comes immediately towards to you.

COME: The Basic Command

'Come' is one of the most basic things you need to teach your Miniature Schnauzer puppy. This command is important for safety reasons, as well as for the puppy to have more freedom. 'Come' let's your dog come near to you and then have off-leash walks without worrying that the dog will run away from you.

If you want your puppy to 'come' to you, make sure you understand why the dog does not want to come. Your dog might be preoccupied with its activities such as playing or chasing other pets.

Chapter Six: Miniature Schnauzer as Show Dogs

Here are the steps on how you can teach your dog to come:

- Tell the puppy, "Come, (dog's name)!"
- Show your dog the treat.
- Reward the puppy when it comes near you.
- When your dog has eaten the treat, pet and praise your dog.
- Repeat the training, but this time, moves backward.
- When your puppy is constantly returning to you when you have commanded it, eliminate the treat, but rely more on praise.

You should do the training session in short period but in multiple attempts. Use different parts of the house and almost try to play hide and seek. If your dog is uninterested in playing this, make sure you are not training when stressed out or after eating. Always remember to reward and give a lot of attention when the puppy has responded.

When your dog has already mastered this, you can add distractions, such as telling them to come to unknown territory or outside.

Chapter Six: Miniature Schnauzer as Show Dogs

SIT: The Second Command

Sitting is a natural behaviour; you need to take advantage whenever the dog is sitting:

- When you notice that your dog is coming to a sitting position, say 'sit'. This allows your dog to realize that SIT means putting its bottom down on the ground.

- You can also encourage your dog using treats.

- Sit on the floor with the puppy, and hold the treat above its head, then backwards. Your dog will raise its nose to cause itself to sit.

- When the back quarters are lowered, say 'sit' and give the treat when your dog's butt is on the floor.

Just like the first training, make sure that these training sessions are only short. Say 'sit' when you notice that your dog is beginning to sit even when outside the training session. You can mix 'come' with 'sit' to make your dog think.

Remember to praise the dog verbally and through petting. When your dog gets better at sitting, remove the treats and increase the physical and verbal praise.

Chapter Six: Miniature Schnauzer as Show Dogs

LAY DOWN: THE THIRD COMMAND

Here is the way to teach your dog to lie down:

- Teach your dog to sit, place the treat on your fingers then on the ground in front of the dog. Your dog will lie on his stomach.

- If it does not respond positively, stand up and gently move the dog's front legs while saying the word 'down'.

- Reward the dog with praise and food.

- Your dog will stand up immediately; it may need a lot of time to get used to the idea of laying down. However, it will soon master this command and encourage the dog to stay longer.

STAY: The Final Basic Command

If your dog has successfully learned how to come, sit, and lay down, it is also important for them to know the word 'stay'. This can be a way to teach your dog to stay:

- Have your dog sit or lay down.

- Say 'Stay'. You can pair this up with a hand signal such as 'stop'

- Increase space and time. Your dog will get used to this idea and may stay longer overtime.

Chapter Six: Miniature Schnauzer as Show Dogs

These are some reminders you need to remember if you want to train your Miniature Schnauzer. You might think this is a difficult task, but you need to remember to make it enjoyable for both you and your pet. Have fun!

Chapter Seven: Miniature Schnauzer as Show Dogs

Miniature Schnauzers are a get breed to show. They are small dogs with big attitudes that will surely wow the crowd in no time. However, there are rules and regulations you need to follow in order to make your pet into the wonderful show dog it intends to be.

Entering and winning shows are not easy tasks. You need to give time, effort, and preparation that need cooperation for both you and your pet. However, this task is also a rewarding experience. Let us dive in to know more about the wonderful way of showmanship.

Chapter Seven: Miniature Schnauzer as Show Dogs

The Miniature Schnauzer Standard

There are many variations and kinds of a Miniature Schnauzer. However, your Schnauzer should conform to the standard given by the American Kennel Club (AKC) or the Canadian Kennel Club (CKC). The Miniature Schnauzer belongs to the terrier group for the AKC and CKC while it is in the Utility group for other kennel club. Here is the breed standard for our Miniature Schnauzer:

✓ HEAD

- The Miniature Schnauzer should have a rectangular in shape head which should appear to be strong
- Your dog needs to have a keen intelligent look.
- There must be a slight tapering from the eyes to the ears, and starting from the eyes up to the tip of the nose.
- Miniature Schnauzer's skull top needs to be flat and its forehead must be unwrinkled.
- Its muzzle is blunt and strong, that is covered with a lot of layer of whiskers.
- Its teeth have a scissors bite and should be strong and even.
- It must have deep - set small dark brown oval eyes.

Chapter Seven: Miniature Schnauzer as Show Dogs

- The ears could be natural or cropped. The cropped ears must come to a tip and symmetrical while natural ears must fold to a V-shape and the fold must be near the dog's skull.

✓ NECK

- Your dog's neck must be in proportionate and should be strong.
- The neck should have an arch from the back part of the skull up to its body.

✓ BODY

- Its body must be deep and have a pronounced brisket.
- Your dog's body do not need to have a cut up into the back; it should have a slight angle towards the back of its rib.
- There should be a minimal drop from the withers up to the back of the tail and its backline must be straight.
- Miniature Schnauzer's tail must be high and carried erect on the back.

Chapter Seven: Miniature Schnauzer as Show Dogs

✓ **FOREQUARTERS**

- Its front legs must be parallel and straight from all directions.
- The elbows must not appear to be sticking out of its side however it should be near the body.
- Your dog must have a muscular and powerful shoulder. Other than that, it should be going the back not going to the chest.
- Its leg must have a motion and can extend fully forward during any task.
- It must have very compact feet and can resemble a round feet that is like a cat.
- It should have black pads.

✓ **HINDQUARTERS**

- Its hindquarters must muscular looking and are bent at the stifles.
- The Miniature Schnauzer's hocks needs to extend beyond the tail when the dog is standing while in a show.
- The back legs should parallel to each other when viewed from any direction.

Chapter Seven: Miniature Schnauzer as Show Dogs

✓ COAT

- The coat is thick and double, with longer furnishing on the legs.
- The ears, head, neck, chest, tail and body coat is plucked or stripped for showing.
- The hair should not appear silky or slick. A coat that is too soft or too smooth will be considered a fault.

✓ COLOR

- There are only three recognized colors; o black, o black and silver, and o salt and pepper.
- There are several slight color variations depending on the color scheme, but there should not be white striping or spotting, except small white patch allowed on the center of the chest in the black Miniature Schnauzer.

✓ GAIT

- The Miniature Schnauzer is judged in a trot, and the legs should move straight forward and backwards easily.
- Your dog must have a fluid looking smooth gait.

Chapter Seven: Miniature Schnauzer as Show Dogs

- Your dog must have spirited and alert temperament. Other than that, it should be attentive and obedient to the handler and audience.

DISQUALIFYING FACTORS

- There are still things that could disqualify your pet Miniature Schnauzer from the show ring. These are:
- The dog is smaller than 12 inches or higher than 14 inches.
- White markings are not allowed for Miniature Schnauzer, except for a small patch on the black Miniature Schnauzer.
- Too aggressive or timid.

The best Miniature Schnauzer on the show ring is based on the dog's ability and its physical ability to meet standards. There are several faults that would cause your dog to lose points during the competition; this will prevent them from being champions.

If you are only planning to breed your Miniature Schnauzer, it is okay to not follow the breed standards we have given. There are many wonderful crossbreeds that do not place first in competitions.

Chapter Seven: Miniature Schnauzer as Show Dogs

These are some reminders you need to know if you want to enter your dog as show dogs. Remember that you need to provide proper documents before entering any competition.

Chapter Seven: Miniature Schnauzer as Show Dogs

Chapter Eight: Grooming My Pet Miniature Schnauzer

A great feature of your Miniature Schnauzer is its beard fur, smart looking brows, and long leg hairs. These features are always seen on the Miniature Schnauzer together with its intelligence and athletic set-up. This breed is has a wiry hair and sheds a little, so it is a great choice for anyone who have allergies to dog hair.

Although the shedding is only minimal, there will still be hair loss, so you still need to groom your Miniature Schnauzer daily to eliminate the problem and keep your dog's coat in good shape and free from any knots.

Chapter Eight: Grooming My Pet Miniature Schnauzer

The fur is not the only thing you need to groom for your pet. There are other things that you need to deal with. In this chapter, we will discuss it to you.

WHITE TEETH

Unlike other small breeds, Miniature Schnauzers do not contract gum and tooth diseases. You can keep your dog's teeth in shape through everyday brushing.

This is only a simple procedure, you only need to use a finger sleeve and a small amount of doggy toothpaste and massage the gums and teeth to remove tartar.

If your dog has already gotten use to this, this will eliminate a very expensive trip to the vet.

SHORT NAILS

It is important to cut your Miniature Schnauzer's nails or claws; this is to prevent damaged furniture and sore feed.

You can use a guillotine type dog nail clipper and very gently remove the nail tip. You should not cut the nail too quick, or your dog's nail will breed and hurt your dog.

If you do not know how to cut your dog's nail, you can seek assistance to your vet or a professional groomer; you watch how he or she works, so you can do it at home.

Chapter Eight: Grooming My Pet Miniature Schnauzer

GROOMING

Your Miniature Schnauzer's long hair or furnishings, especially on its legs, are prone to matting. You need to brush the hair daily and brush thoroughly on the parts where there is longer hair, such as in its beard or belly to prevent knots.

You can start by combing the hair upwards at the leg top and, you need to use a pin brush, brush it down. This is to ensure that you are not only brushing the long hair's surface, but also to remove any tangles or deep mats.

Pay a special attention to the area around the armpit on belly front, this is a sensitive part of the dog but is also a great problem for the matting.

Groom the eyebrows and beard carefully using a comb. You always need to brush forward but avoid the eyes and the mouth. If you plan to clip or cut the hair on the face, you need to cut or clip with hair growth, not against. If you cut or clip against the hair growth direction, this can pull more hair or even burn the skin and leave open areas for possible infection.

The hair on the head is needed to be clipped close to the skull, and eyebrows and ears hair are just shaped with

Chapter Eight: Grooming My Pet Miniature Schnauzer

scissors and left long. You can leave alone the beard, as long as it not unruly.

Many Miniature Schnauzer owners bring their dogs to a professional groomer once or twice a month, and just do basic clipping and trimming at home.

Many owners want to keep the dog trimmed very close so they do not have to worry about its fur. However, you can't enter your dog in many contests if you have cut it too close.

BATHING

You need to keep the natural oils on the Miniature Schnauzer's lengthy coat as possible. Your dog should only be bathed when necessary. If you need to bathe the dog, you need to use a dog shampoo and avoid using human products.

Remember the human shampoo pH level can be harmful to dogs' skin and coat; it could lead to problems such as possible hair loss and scratching.

EARS AND EYES

If you want to groom your Miniature Schnauzer's ears and eyes, you just need a damp soft cloth and gently

Chapter Eight: Grooming My Pet Miniature Schnauzer

wipe the eyes. This method removes any junk or debris and stops the problem with accumulated matter in the eyes.

Your vet needs to examine the significant staining or tearing if it is present. If their ears are not cropped, your Miniature Schnauzer will have difficulty with the wax build-up in the ear. The inside of a damp and warm ear is a perfect place where bacteria could grow, because its ears have natural folds.

You just need to wipe the inside of the ear of a warm cloth to prevent problems and remove accumulation. There are many solutions available from your groomer or vet if you notice that there is a waxy discharge and help remove the build-up. Aside from this, if your dog has a lot of hair in its ear canal, you may need to pluck. If you don't want to do this task, you may ask your groomer for help. Do not use pointy objects or any tweezers near your dog's ear canal because this can permanently damage the dog ear if he or she has flinched or twitched.

If you frequently brush your Miniature Schnauzer, it will get used to the routine and this will prevent tangling of its hair. You need to start this habit as early as possible.

Chapter Eight: Grooming My Pet Miniature Schnauzer

BATHING MY DOG

Even though you have kept your dog neat and clean, you still need to give your dog its needed bath time. You need to start this habit as a dog; this task will eliminate the issue when the dog gets older.

Since the Miniature Schnauzer is only a small dog, you can bathe it in a bathtub or sink. It is still according to the dog's preference if it wants bathing and water. Ask your vet if your dog is water lovin' or not. If not, there are a lot of commercially available powders that will work to quickly deodorize and freshen up your dog's coat.

Take great caution when you use these powders to avoid contact with the ears, eyes, or mouth. Your dog might be sensitive to the perfumes and chemicals in some powders, shampoos, or soaps, use this first on a small area of your dog before you treat it to the whole dog.

Here are the correct steps in bathing your dog:

- Remove all foreign matter from your dog's coat. There might be a lot of foreign matter as your dog has long hair. Some small objects or twigs may cause tangling during bath time; you need to remove these things ahead of time to save your patience and effort.

Chapter Eight: Grooming My Pet Miniature Schnauzer

- Prepare your bathtub, sink or other water container, with luke-warm water and gently place your dog in it. Remember, do not use water that is deeper than the top of the animal's legs or the bottom of their belly.

- You need to use your arms and hands to support your Miniature Schnauzer until it is not struggling and comfortable in the situation. Avoid any slips and falls anytime during bath time. Gently place one hand on the back of your dog's neck or its stomach, especially for small breed like the Miniature Schnauzer. You need to praise and talk to your dog in an assuring tone. Aside from this, praise your dog if it stands still.

- A hose and shower nozzle is an ideal way to wet your dog and then rinse it off with a shampoo. You need to use warm to touch water, do not use too hot or too cold water for your dog. Use the gentlest settle if there is an adjustment setting from that will adjust its water output from the nozzle.

- Slowly pour water from a plastic pitcher or any other plastic container to your dog's back, start with its tail and move towards the neck. Do not us any glass object that might break off during the process. Calm your dog if it becomes too nervous or tries to move

Chapter Eight: Grooming My Pet Miniature Schnauzer

before you do any more procedures. You should not pour water from your dog's head, because this will frighten your animal.

- If the dog is already wet from neck to tail, put a great quality of pet shampoo and lather. Use a free hand to support your dog and the other one to lather it. Since your dog is only a small dog, you can just do the task alone.

- When you have shampooed completely your dog, rinse it thoroughly using warm water. Start from the top of the dog up to the bottom and make sure that all of the shampoo is removed.

- Finish the bath with hair conditioner/good skin conditioner that is meant for dogs. Then, rinse thoroughly.

Your Miniature Schnauzer may want to shake, which well depends on its dog enthusiasm, that can be very messy. Rinse the dog immediately then remove the dog from the water and dry it with fluffy towels.

Support the dog by keeping your hand on the back of its neck to prevent the shaking or minimize the amount of shaking until you can completely towel dry the dog. Use a

Chapter Eight: Grooming My Pet Miniature Schnauzer

soft washcloth that is rinsed with warm water for the ears and face after the bath.

Remember, do not use any conditioner or shampoo on the eyes, ears, nose, and face, because these areas are very sensitive. Your dog will want to run and roll outside of the house after the bath. This dog's activity will undo all of your hard work. You need to keep your dog confined on one space until its coat is dried completely.

You can dry your dog with a hair dryer, especially its outer and inner coat; this will prevent diseases and skin irritations. Do not use a human hair dryer unless you have a lot setting. High and medium heat on regular hair dryers will be very hot for your dogs; this could cause skin damage and problems with the next bath session with your beloved dog. Your local pet store might sell special hair dryers that have low temperature setting with different speeds.

After it has taken some baths, your dog might like this task and look forward to it in the future. You can increase the dog's desire for a bath time using positive reinforcement such as rewarding the dog of its great behavior during bath time or even doing something special with the dog.

Chapter Eight: Grooming My Pet Miniature Schnauzer

EAR CARE FOR DOGS

Most healthy Miniature Schnauzer will encounter problems with their ears. There are several conditions that might arise with their ears.

These are some of the general conditions that you will see if your dogs have ear problems:

- Frequent scratching of the ears
- Scaly appearance or tumor in the ears
- Frequent and repeated shaking of the head
- Ears appear red and are sensitive to the touch
- Foul smell or discharge from the ears

You should immediately check with your veterinarian if your dog has exhibited any of these signs. Causes for these symptoms are water in the ear, ear mites, or any other condition that might need specific medical intervention. If the condition becomes very severe, this could lead to hearing loss and even your dog's death.

GENERAL EAR CARE

You need to know your dog's breed to fully know and understand and understand how much attention you need to give, especially to its ear.

Chapter Eight: Grooming My Pet Miniature Schnauzer

Dogs with ears that are covered with a longer art of the ear or ear flaps will have a lot more complications with ear problems than those dogs with open ears; the reason for this phenomenon is that dogs with ear flaps lack enough air circulation and accumulate a lot wax.

Dogs with open ears have a clear air circulation so that the wax is expelled from the ears regularly.

The first sign for the wax accumulation is a greasy discharge from its ear, along with the pungent waxy smell. There will be a dark colored discharge, this is a clear sign or ear canker and may need to be treated by the vet. If your dog has a light or clear ear discharge, this can be cleansed using a commercially prepared ear solution and the cotton ball.

You just need to soak the pad or cotton ball in the solution, make sure to squeeze any excess moisture and gently apply to the inside of the ear. Do not push the cotton inside of the ear canal or allow the solution to enter the ear canal. Do not use a Q tip or any other sharp object inside the ear, your dog might have a permanent hearing loss if there is a sudden movement of your dog's head.

Sometime there might be wax built up in the farther part of the ear canal. You can consult your vet and ask him or her to irrigate the ear canal and remove the wax. This

Chapter Eight: Grooming My Pet Miniature Schnauzer

procedure needs to be done several times if there are a lot of build-ups. Remember, irrigation should only be done by a vet or other professional animal health specialist.

Dogs with long hairs in their ears may cause a lot of irritation with an increase of redness and itching on the ears. You need to remove or trim long hairs if it will become a problem for your dog's ear.

Water in the dog's ear canal will not only cause a discharge, but it could further lead to bacteria growth in the ear canal. If you see any irritation, stop the cleaning activity and immediately call and schedule an interview with your vet.

Professional groomers will also regularly clean your dog's ear when it is bathe, aside from cleaning, most groomer will let you know if there are nay discharge or problem with your dog's ear. Ear mites are very common in dogs; this will require treatment for several weeks.

If you own more than one dog and it has mites, you need to monitor the other dogs as the mites easily travel between and among your dogs. It is very difficult to find the mites, but it can be easily seen if the wax from the Miniature Schnauzer's ear is thinly spread on the paper. The spots in wax are the ear mites.

Chapter Eight: Grooming My Pet Miniature Schnauzer

YEARLY CHECK-UPS

Even if you dislike bringing your dog to a groomer, you still need to check the dog ears for any discharge and changes in their behaviour such as head shaking or scratching.

Your vet could easily check the discharge or if there is strong odor as soon as possible. If your dog has developed the wax build up, your dog's ear must be cleaned with a cotton ball and a solution. Aside from this, you need to check the dog's ear and hearing during yearly visits.

Old Miniature Schnauzers may have a decrease in the hearing area, but this is only normal, but it also means that they need to clean their ear more frequently. You need to follow your vet's advice.

These are some reminders when you want to groom your pet, you might be overwhelmed with a lot of steps, but you will surely learn how to manage the time and look for the best procedure for grooming your Miniature Schnauzer

Chapter Eight: Grooming My Pet Miniature Schnauzer

Chapter Nine: My Miniature Schnauzer's Medical Needs

Taking care of your Miniature Schnauzer is not that easy. You start with its puppyhood up until the day of its death. You need to know all of these things because you might encounter these things in the future. It is better to know these things than know nothing at all.

In here, we will give different things or pointers to look out for regarding the medical needs of your dog. These are just some of the daily reminders that we have listed down to make sure that your puppy will be safe and healthy.

Chapter Nine: My Mini Schnauzer's Medical Needs
PREVENT THE SICKNESS, RATHER THAN CURING IT

Just like the other things in our life, we need to address several problems before they even arise, this will save effort, time, and money especially in our thrifty pockets. This holds true even for our Miniature Schnauzer. However, your dog is a living, loving, and breathing being that is a member of our family. If your Miniature Schnauzer contracts any diseases, you and your family will become stressed out due to the fact that something is wrong with your family.

You will need to spend time to plan out and track your Miniature Schnauzer's well-being and health, take note of the different changes in dog's behaviour and performance which will indicate health concerns that might need a trip to the vet.

DAILY AND WEEKLY

You need to look out for these things on a daily and weekly basis:

- If your Miniature Schnauzer is not interacting with other dogs, people in the family, or wants to stay alone. If you have raised your dog to be alone, this will not be major concern; however, a normally social dog would really want to interact with other people and things.

Chapter Nine: My Mini Schnauzer's Medical Needs

- Look at how your dog moves inside and outside of the house, make sure that the dog is not stiff or have certain change in gait. Note the changes from day to day to see if the stiffness disappears, stays, or even gets the worse. Miniature Schnauzers, just like us, can strain themselves that may result to stiffness. This sickness may likely occur to the older dog, so, try to limit stressful and strenuous activity for them. See if your older dog can keep up, even if it is very painful for them.

- Notice how your dog eats. Note how they chew their food and not simply gulping food down. Miniature Schnauzer might gulp down their food if they feel that they have not eaten enough and constantly hungry, or if there is something wrong with their teeth and may find chewing difficult and painful.

- Watch if there has any blood in the saliva, especially around the mouth during eating.

- If your dog is very hungry, you need to increase how much you feed your dog, or feed it several small meals a day rather than giving it a big meal one time.

- See how much water your dog is drinking throughout the day. Drinking too much water could be a sign of

Chapter Nine: My Mini Schnauzer's Medical Needs

several health conditions. Drinking then vomiting the water should be well noted, and you need to rush your dog to the vet for assistance. You can detect a lot of conditions for the digestive tract, kidney, and liver by how much water your dog has consumed. If your dog is not drinking enough, it may have a kidney problem; it could be toxic especially if your dog will stop urinating.

- Make sure that your Miniature Schnauzer has access to adequate fresh clean water, because your dog should not and will not drink fouled or unclean water.

- Note if there is an irregular activity in bowel movement or urination. Your dog may have diarrhea if you have changed its feeding amount or if there are many table scraps fed to the dog. This could be a symptom of a life threatening and serious disease such as the parvovirus.

- If your dog still has diarrhea after two or three days, you should bring your dog to the vet. Your vet may need you to bring stool sample to diagnose and know what the problem is. Aside from this, intestinal parasites or some worms might be visible in the stool. Hookworms and roundworms could be fatal to the

Chapter Nine: My Mini Schnauzer's Medical Needs

puppies which can also be transmitted to the humans. These worms could lead to anemia and overall poor health and coat condition.

WEEKLY TO MONTHLY

- You need to weigh your Miniature Schnauzer at least once a month. Overweight dogs, like their counterpart, have great risks for medical conditions. If you have weighed your dog, you need to monitor if your dog is eating properly and will not be overeating. Notice if the dog is gaining weight, so you need to try decrease the food at small amount, forgo the treats and table scraps but increase the exercise.

- Exercise with your dog and notice if there are any changes in your dog's general fitness health and stamina.

- Remember to trim your Miniature Schnauzer's nails, make sure to clean the eyes and ears, and check their skin condition at least once a month. Run your hands throughout the dog's body to see if there are any growths, tumors, and any swelling. Note also if the dog's skin is dry or scaly hair, or if there are signs of fleas, mites, to fully know how to treat it or at least manage it.

Chapter Nine: My Mini Schnauzer's Medical Needs

- Regularly visit your vet for your Miniature Schnauzer, even if it is an adult or puppy. Make sure you follow all the vaccination schedules and report if there will be any changes in your dog's condition or behavior especially during the critical 24-48 hours.

Make sure you prevent things before it even happen, this hold true even for our dear pet. They do not know how to talk for themselves; they rely on how much attention you give them to know if they need a change in environment or if they are not feeling well. Resolving these things earlier will catch more problems rather than leading them to larger and bigger complications.

DENTAL CARE

Although you might think this is strange, you still need to take care of your Miniature Schnauzer's teeth throughout its life. Many people think that a dog can take care of its own teeth. This can hold true if you only feed your dog all natural ingredients and food that they would have eaten if they have remained as wild animals.

Domesticated animals eat a lot of chemical and food that are never a part of nature. They are susceptible to dental health issues in the same way we are. Aside from this, your dog lives longer in our home rather than in nature, so your senior dog will benefit greatly if you will give them great dental care in their lives.

TEETH

Puppies will start getting their teeth at the age of three to four weeks. They will have 28 puppy teeth; these teeth will be replaced with 42 permanent adult teeth during its 4th month. Dogs have four different types of teeth:

- Molars – used for chewing
- Premolars – hold and break up the food
- Canines – used to hold and tear the food into small pieces
- Incisors – cut and nibble

Many vets assume that around 80% of dogs of the age of three develop a form of gum disease. This will cause a lot of problems for the dog, such as chewing which will lead to digestive problem.

Just like us, not taking care of the teeth will cause the teeth to be easily damaged or start to fall out. This will get worse as the dog ages, which could even lead to fatal health conditions.

Chapter Nine: My Mini Schnauzer's Medical Needs
HOW TO TAKE CARE OF THE CANINE TEETH

It is not necessary to brush your Miniature Schnauzer's teeth every day, but it is 'til a good idea to do this task at least twice a week, or every two days. You may need to use finger brush; this will serve like a little sleeve that fits well over your finger. It has a texture that will provide a scrubbing action and will not painfully and accidentally bump your dog's gums during cleaning. Aside from the finger brush, you need to use doggy toothpaste. Just like the soap, do not use human toothpaste because it is not correctly formulated for the dogs, and it has a very unpleasant taste for them.

You need to start this routine at a very young age, which will help them get used to the procedure. If you plan to show your dog, it may require more brushing to keep their teeth healthy and bright.

BONES

You can use a good, raw, beef marrow or knuckle bone as a way to help your dog clean its teeth. Do not give cooked bone or a straight flat bone, because this may cause splinter and other health issues.

If the bone is beginning to shred or getting smaller enough to be swallowed, remove it from your dog, as it may cause damages.

Chapter Nine: My Mini Schnauzer's Medical Needs

Your butcher will save knuckle bones if you ask them nicely. There are some commercially available 'tarter bones'. These kinds of bones are great for all sizes as they come in several thicknesses. You need to take great care to remove the bone as they will become very small for the dog and very easy to ingest.

CONCERNS

While you are brushing your Miniature Schnauzer's teeth, you need to look for any signs of inflammation, bleeding, or redness along the gum line. This could be normal if your puppy changing to its adult teeth, but not very normal for adult Miniature Schnauzer after its sixth month of being.

Look for heavy deposits of tartar along gum lines or even extending to their teeth. It is a yellow to brown color and may not come off easily with simple brushing.

If the tartar builds - up is very severe, you need to have it removed by the vet. Scaling is what this process is called. This will require your dog to be anesthetized, which is a costly procedure.

Although your dog does not have a sweet smelling breath, it is still important for your vet to check if that foul smelling breath is a sign of a serious illness. Foul smelling breath could be an indication of a digestive or dental

Chapter Nine: My Mini Schnauzer's Medical Needs

problem, so you need to know these issues as early as possible.

MEDICAL CARE

Unlike other dogs, your Miniature Schnauzer only has a few health concerns that you need to worry about.

Your Miniature Schnauzer is a very robust and health dog, and could live up to the 14 years, and will remain playful and active until their senior year.

There are still diseases that could be contracted by the Miniature Schnauzer; you need to look out for the symptoms for you to easily identify what is the sickness about.

WEIGHT GAIN

Miniature Schnauzers are very active dog especially when they have the opportunity to run, walk, or play even for days. If they will not be given this opportunity, they would just sit on the couch all day long.

Overweight dogs are more prone to skeletal or muscle problems, as well as cardiovascular problems. You need to monitor how much your dog needs and provide them regular active exercises. Do not give human food or table scraps and only feed them premium dog food provide proper nutrition.

Chapter Nine: My Mini Schnauzer's Medical Needs

The aforementioned things are just some of the medical things that you need to know about your Miniature Schnauzer. These are just some of the daily reminders that deal with medical concerns. Make sure you still research on common dog illness and consult your vet about it.

Chapter Nine: My Mini Schnauzer's Medical Needs

Quick Summary and Care Sheet

We have already gathered a lot of things about the Miniature Schnauzer, you need, now, to go outside and get your own Miniature Schnauzer and use the things you have learned! You can still get more information through other website or guide books to further enhance your knowledge about the Miniature Schnauzer. The knowledge you will gain will further give you information about the breed and how to give it a happy and healthy life. In this final chapter, we will sum up the important information we have discussed throughout the different chapters, these information are important for you and your Miniature Schnauzer.

Basic Information for Miniature Schnauzer

Origin: Germany

Pedigree:

Breed Size: small size

Body Type and Appearance: The Miniature Schnauzer can be seen as 'square' in proportion. The length of their body is almost equal to the height.

Group: classified as Terrier Group in the American Kennel Club (AKC) as well as the Canadian Kennel Club (CKC); classified as utility group in other kennel club

Height: 30 cm - 36 cm for both male and female.

Weight: 5.4 - 8.2 kg for female, 5.4 - 9.1 kg for male

Coat Length: thick and double

Coat Texture: wiry and fairly coarse

Color: brindle, white, black, fawn, blue, red

Temperament: fearless, spirited, obedient, alert, intelligent, friendly, friendly, smart, active

Strangers: will depend on the training you will give

Other Dogs: some might attack, some might be friendly

Other Pets: depends well on the training of the owner

Training: loves to be trained by their humans

Exercise Needs: needs daily exercise

Health Conditions: almost all are healthy but may be affected by the following illnesses: von willebrand's disease, anesthesia sensitivity, deafness, and other eye diseases.

Lifespan: average 12 to 14 years

Home Requirements

Recommended Accessories: harness, dog bed, food/water dishes, grooming supplies crate, toys, collar, leash

Collar and Harness: sized by weight

Grooming Supplies: nail clipper, comb, glove for the owner

Grooming Frequency: twice month

Energy Level: alert little creatures that will certainly get its way

Exercise Requirements: daily exercise is needed to remove excess energy

Crate: you can use this as a mode of transportation

Crate Size: medium to large

Food/Water: preferably stainless steel, ceramic bowls, or high quality plastics

Toys: give enough toys as not to have a bored Miniature Schnauzer

Training: hard to train, but once you have established authority, you can control it

Nutritional Needs

Nutritional Needs: water, vitamins, minerals, carbohydrate, protein, fats

Calorie Needs: enough calories is only needed as they may get fat easily

Amount to Feed (puppy): you can do trial and error method, or even consult your vet for the proper feeding guide

Amount to Feed (adult): slowly change the food frequency when it ages

Important Ingredients: fresh animal protein (chicken, turkey, beef, lamb, eggs), digestible carbohydrates (rice, oats, barley), animal fats

Important Minerals: calcium, magnesium, manganese phosphorus, potassium iron, copper

Important Vitamins: , Vitamin D, Vitamin A, Vitamin B-12, Vitamin C.

Glossary of Pup Terms

Abundism – Referring to a pup that has markings more prolific than is normal.

Acariasis – A type of mite infection.

ACF – Australian Pup Federation

Affix – A puptery name that follows the pup's registered name; puptery owner, not the breeder of the pup.

Agouti – A type of natural coloring pattern in which individual hairs have bands of light and dark coloring.

Ailurophile – A person who loves pups.

Albino – A type of genetic mutation which results in little to no pigmentation, in the eyes, skin, and coat.

Allbreed – Referring to a show that accepts all breeds or a judge who is qualified to judge all breeds.

Alley Pup – A non-pedigreed pup.

Alter – A desexed pup; a male pup that has been neutered or a female that has been spayed.

Amino Acid – The building blocks of protein; there are 22 types for pups, 11 of which can be synthesized and 11 which must come from the diet (see essential amino acid).

Anestrus – The period between estrus cycles in a female pup.

Any Other Variety (AOV) – A registered pup that doesn't conform to the breed standard.

ASH – American Shorthair, a breed of pup.

Back Cross – A type of breeding in which the offspring is mated back to the parent.

Balance – Referring to the pup's structure; proportional in accordance with the breed standard.

Barring – Describing the tabby's striped markings.

Base Color – The color of the coat.

Bicolor – A pup with patched color and white.

Blaze – A white coloring on the face, usually in the shape of an inverted V.

Bloodline – The pedigree of the pup.

Brindle – A type of coloring, a brownish or tawny coat with streaks of another color.

Castration – The surgical removal of a male pup's testicles.

Pup Show – An event where pups are shown and judged.

Puptery – A registered pup breeder; also, a place where pups may be boarded.

CFA – The Pup Fanciers Association.

Cobby – A compact body type.

Colony – A group of pups living wild outside.

Color Point – A type of coat pattern that is controlled by color point alleles; pigmentation on the tail, legs, face, and ears with an ivory or white coat.

Colostrum – The first milk produced by a lactating female; contains vital nutrients and antibodies.

Conformation – The degree to which a pedigreed pup adheres to the breed standard.

Cross Breed – The offspring produced by mating two distinct breeds.

Dam – The female parent.

Declawing – The surgical removal of the pup's claw and first toe joint.

Developed Breed – A breed that was developed through selective breeding and crossing with established breeds.

Down Hairs – The short, fine hairs closest to the body which keep the pup warm.

DSH – Domestic Shorthair.

Estrus – The reproductive cycle in female pups during which she becomes fertile and receptive to mating.

Fading Pup Syndrome – Pups that die within the first two weeks after birth; the cause is generally unknown.

Feral – A wild, untamed pup of domestic descent.

Gestation – Pregnancy; the period during which the fetuses develop in the female's uterus.

Guard Hairs – Coarse, outer hairs on the coat.

Harlequin – A type of coloring in which there are van markings of any color with the addition of small patches of the same color on the legs and body.

Inbreeding – The breeding of related pups within a closed group or breed.

Kibble – Another name for dry pup food.

Lilac – A type of coat color that is pale pinkish-gray.

Line – The pedigree of ancestors; family tree.

Litter – The name given to a group of pups born at the same time from a single female.

Mask – A type of coloring seen on the face in some breeds.

Matts – Knots or tangles in the pup's fur.

Mittens – White markings on the feet of a pup.

Moggie – Another name for a mixed breed pup.

Mutation – A change in the DNA of a cell.

Muzzle – The nose and jaws of an animal.

Natural Breed – A breed that developed without selective breeding or the assistance of humans.

Neutering – Desexing a male pup.

Open Show – A show in which spectators are allowed to view the judging.

Pads – The thick skin on the bottom of the feet.

Particolor – A type of coloration in which there are markings of two or more distinct colors.

Patched – A type of coloration in which there is any solid color, tabby, or tortoiseshell color plus white.

Pedigree – A purebred pup; the pup's papers showing its family history.

Pet Quality – A pup that is not deemed of high enough standard to be shown or bred.

Piebald – A pup with white patches of fur.

Points – Also color points; markings of contrasting color on the face, ears, legs, and tail.

Pricked – Referring to ears that sit upright.

Purebred – A pedigreed pup.

Queen – An intact female pup.

Roman Nose – A type of nose shape with a bump or arch.

Scruff – The loose skin on the back of a pup's neck.

Selective Breeding – A method of modifying or improving a breed by choosing pups with desirable traits.

Senior – A pup that is more than 5 but less than 7 years old.

Sire – The male parent of a pup.

Solid – Also self; a pup with a single coat color.

Spay – Desexing a female pup.

Stud – An intact male pup.

Tabby – A type of coat pattern consisting of a contrasting color over a ground color.

Tom Pup – An intact male pup.

Tortoiseshell – A type of coat pattern consisting of a mosaic of red or cream and another base color.

Tri-Color – A type of coat pattern consisting of three distinct colors in the coat.

Tuxedo – A black and white pup.

Unaltered – A pup that has not been desexed.

Index

A

accessories 23, 26, 36, 43, 44, 48, 107
active 35, 40
adopt 36
adopting 2
age 5, 20, 25, 61, 88, 109
alfalfa 52, 61, 62, 63, 113, 114
altered 20
angora 3
animal movement license 19
antibiotics 98, 102
antiseptic 26, 72, 76
APHIS 19, 130
appearance 3

B

baby 5, 7, 34, 35, 36, 40, 41, 42, 61, 64, 69, 100
back 6, 54, 77, 89, 107
bacteria 24, 46, 50, 76, 101, 106
bathing 71, 74
bed 23
bedding 27, 28, 45, 48, 50, 68, 94, 105, 107, 108, 131
behavior 66, 92
belly 5, 67
birth 5, 6, 61, 68
birthing 5
bladder 96
bleach 107
blood 6, 75, 94, 95
body 4, 6, 7, 41, 54, 75, 80, 99, 104
bodyweight 27, 58, 59, 62, 114
bowls 23, 24, 48
box 5, 6, 26, 30, 41, 46, 67, 68, 69, 96, 113
breathing 94, 103

breed 2, 4, 5, 8, 18, 23, 25, 27, 29, 30, 33, 34, 35, 44, 48, 65, 66, 70, 79, 80, 87, 88, 92, 115
breed standard 79, 81
breeder 33, 34, 35, 40
breeding 2, 5, 24, 34, 35, 36, 65, 66
breeds 3, 4, 20, 21, 24, 35, 71, 74, 80
broken 4
brush 26, 72, 74, 88
budget 25, 26, 29

C

cage 20, 24, 26, 28, 36, 41, 43, 45, 46, 47, 48, 51, 54, 66, 67, 96, 97, 99, 104, 106, 107, 112, 115
care 30, 75, 92, 129, 131
pup litter 50
pups 21, 25, 30, 108
causes 93, 96, 99
characteristics 3
chest 54
chewing 44
children 2, 5, 31
chin 4
cleaning 88
clipping 23
coat 3, 4, 5, 6, 7, 4, 14, 71, 72, 75, 99, 105, 111
collar 26
coloring 3
colors 4
comb 72
condition 6, 35, 72, 94, 96, 99, 105
conjunctivitis 101
convulsions 94, 100
costs 23, 26, 27, 28
courtship 66

D

dangerous 21, 47, 102

defepupe 51
diagnosis 92, 99
diarrhea 40
diet 2, 27, 30, 47, 57, 59, 61, 63, 69, 77, 92, 114, 131
digestion 57, 60
discharge 41, 101, 103
diseases 47, 93, 106, 108, 129
disinfect 104, 107
disorientation 101
docile 21, 30
doe 5, 66, 67, 68, 69, 115
dogs 21, 25, 30, 108

E

ears 3, 41, 71, 75, 95, 101, 108, 115
embryos 67, 115
energy 5
exercise 5, 43, 44, 46, 112
export 19
eyes 41

F

feeding 60, 69
female 4, 20, 66, 67, 114
fever 75, 93, 94, 95, 103
fiber 19, 50, 57, 58, 61, 77, 113
fluid 98, 103
food 4, 6, 7, 23, 24, 27, 28, 48, 60, 77, 89, 94, 98, 107, 113
fruit 59, 62, 114

G

games 44
genes 6
grooming 4, 6, 23, 26, 28, 30, 71, 72, 75, 88, 89, 106
grooming tools 72

guard hairs 3, 4, 6, 7

H

habitat 2, 44, 106
hair 3, 6, 68, 69, 96, 104
handling 43
head 3, 7, 76, 100, 101, 104
head tilt 100, 101
health 2, 27, 34, 35, 71
health problems 2, 92, 93
healthy 27, 28, 33, 35, 40, 58, 63, 69, 106, 114
history 33
hutch 24

I

illness 41, 92, 105, 106
import 19
inbreeding 67
incisors 76
infection 76, 95, 96, 98, 101, 102, 103, 105
infectious 93, 101
inflammation 41, 93, 96, 97, 102
information 33, 34
initial costs 23
intact 4
intelligent 4, 15, 112

J

judging 89

K

kindling 5, 70, 115
pups 115

L

leafy greens	58, 114
legs	4, 6, 7, 104
lesions	99, 104
lethargic	41
lethargy	94, 95, 103
license	18, 19, 33
lifespan	5
litter	4, 26, 27, 28, 30, 32, 36, 40, 43, 46, 49, 51, 52, 64, 68, 69, 96, 113, 131

M

male	4, 6, 20, 66, 114, 115
malnutrition	104
marking	3, 66
materials	24, 46
mating	66, 67, 68
mats	74
meat	5, 7, 19
medipupions	103, 104
microchipping	23
milk	6, 61, 62, 70, 114, 115
mites	105, 108

N

nails	6, 71, 75
neck	6, 105
nervous	21
nest	5, 6, 68, 69, 113
nesting box	68, 69
neuter	23
neutered	25
noise	7, 47, 112
nose	4
nutrients	57, 58, 61, 69
nutrition	4

nutritional needs 57

O

offspring 4, 6
organization 3, 87
outdoor 47, 112

P

pair 20, 66, 77
palpate 67
parasites 47, 96, 106, 108
pattern 6
permit 18, 19
pet 27, 41
pet store 33, 35
pets 5, 7, 14, 18, 19, 21, 53, 111, 129
play 41
pregnancy 66
pregnant 5, 6, 67
prize 89
probiotics 102
problems 42
pros and cons 29
protein 58, 61, 113
purchase 23, 26, 34, 40, 57, 113

Q

qualifipupions 80
quick 75

R

rabies 19
recovery 93

registration 34
regulations 18, 19, 87
reproductive 101
requirements 44
respiratory 101

S

sanitation 96, 97, 99, 102, 104
scent 4
schedule 67, 88, 108
scissors 72
self 89
selling 4, 19
shedding 6, 74
shoulders 3, 6
show 7, 24, 72, 80, 87, 88, 89, 92, 94
showing 2, 79
signs 41
size 7, 20, 27, 45
skin 3, 97, 98, 105, 108
sneezing 101, 103
social 20
socialization 5
solid 7
spay 23
spayed 18, 25, 36
standard 80
stimulation 5, 44
stress 104, 105, 106
supplies 23, 26
surgery 23
swollen 42
symptoms 92, 93, 94, 99, 100, 103

T

tail 6, 105
taming 43

tangles 74
teeth 6, 25, 58, 71, 72, 75, 76, 77
temperament 21
temperature 75
tests 99
texture 6
ticks 95
time 5, 30, 41, 49, 53, 57, 62, 65, 66, 69, 71, 72, 75, 89, 92, 93, 113
timothy hay 50, 58, 113
tips 32
toxic 60
toys 23, 28, 44
train 26, 51
training 5
treatment 2, 92, 93, 94, 95, 97, 98, 100, 102, 103, 104
type 3, 28, 43, 49, 52, 58, 59, 72, 103
types 43

U

unaltered 4
undercoat 3, 4, 5, 6
urinate 51
urine burn 50, 96, 97

V

vaccinations 23, 35
vegetables 27, 57, 58, 59, 60, 62, 113, 114, 131
vet 28
veterinarian 28
veterinary 27
viral 93, 95, 102

W

walk 42
water 23, 24, 48, 57, 88, 89, 94, 98, 107, 113, 114

water bottle 24, 48, 113
weight 63, 94, 103, 114
wound 98

Photo Credits

Page 1 Photo by user Brennan via Flickr.com, https://www.flickr.com/photos/hollandhoodie/642353622/

Page 4 Photo by user Shanna via Flickr.com, https://www.flickr.com/photos/shannaleigh/2490221045/

Page 12 Photo by user Reuben Yau via Flickr.com, https://www.flickr.com/photos/reubenyau/6412444991/

Page 26 Photo by user Alberto Martinez via Flickr.com, https://www.flickr.com/photos/albertma/9085871137/

Page 40 Photo by user essgee51 via Flickr.com, https://www.flickr.com/photos/sg51/4615660090/

Page 46 Photo by user dailyinvention via Flickr.com, https://www.flickr.com/photos/dailyinvention/3576703196/

Page 58 Photo by user Oscar Rohena via Flickr.com, https://www.flickr.com/photos/oscalito/6937051766/

Page 68 Photo by user Ted Murphy via Flickr.com, https://www.flickr.com/photos/tedmurphy/2916770088/

Page 75 Photo by user Fidget Photography via Flickr.com,

https://www.flickr.com/photos/fidget_photography/5598904678/

Page 89 Photo by user via Flickr.com,

Page 100 Photo by user Reuben Yau via Flickr.com,

https://www.flickr.com/photos/reubenyau/7701690602/

References

"Miniature Schnauzer" - Dogtime.com

http://dogtime.com/dog-breeds/miniature-schnauzer#/slide/1

"Miniature Schnauzer Temperament: What's Good About 'Em, What's Bad About 'Em" - YourPureBredPuppy.com

http://www.yourpurebredpuppy.com/reviews/miniatureschnauzers.html

"Miniature Schnauzer" - TheHappyPuppySite.com

https://thehappypuppysite.com/miniature-schnauzer/

"Miniature Schnauzer Dog Breed" – Petwave.com

https://www.petwave.com/Dogs/Breeds/Miniature-Schnauzer.aspx

"The Miniature Schnauzer" - PetHealthNetwork.com

http://www.pethealthnetwork.com/dog-health/dog-breeds/miniature-schnauzer

"Grooming A Miniature Schnauzer the Right Way" – TrainingMiniSchnauzer.com

https://trainingminischnauzer.com/grooming-a-miniature-schnauzer

"Miniature Schnauzer" – AKC.org

https://www.akc.org/dog-breeds/miniature-schnauzer/

Feeding Baby
Cynthia Cherry
978-1941070000

Axolotl
Lolly Brown
978-0989658430

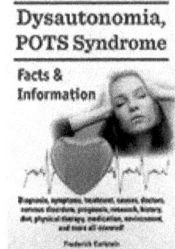

Dysautonomia, POTS Syndrome
Frederick Earlstein
978-0989658485

Degenerative Disc Disease Explained
Frederick Earlstein
978-0989658485

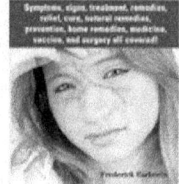

Sinusitis, Hay Fever,
Allergic Rhinitis Explained
Frederick Earlstein
978-1941070024

Wicca
Riley Star
978-1941070130

Zombie Apocalypse
Rex Cutty
978-1941070154

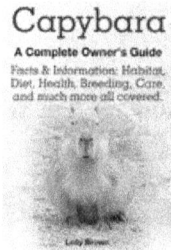

Capybara
Lolly Brown
978-1941070062

Eels As Pets
Lolly Brown
978-1941070167

Scabies and Lice Explained
Frederick Earlstein
978-1941070017

Saltwater Fish As Pets
Lolly Brown
978-0989658461

Torticollis Explained
Frederick Earlstein
978-1941070055

Kennel Cough
Lolly Brown
978-0989658409

Physiotherapist, Physical Therapist
Christopher Wright
978-0989658492

Rats, Mice, and Dormice As Pets
Lolly Brown
978-1941070079

Wallaby and Wallaroo Care
Lolly Brown
978-1941070031

Bodybuilding Supplements
Explained
Jon Shelton
978-1941070239

Demonology
Riley Star
978-19401070314

Pigeon Racing
Lolly Brown
978-1941070307

Dwarf Hamster
Lolly Brown
978-1941070390

Cryptozoology
Rex Cutty
978-1941070406

Eye Strain
Frederick Earlstein
978-1941070369

Inez The Miniature Elephant
Asher Ray
978-1941070353

Vampire Apocalypse
Rex Cutty
978-1941070321

www.ingramcontent.com/pod-product-compliance
Lightning Source LLC
Chambersburg PA
CBHW060836050426
42453CB00008B/709